MW01105023

ccm *l   i   f   e* L I N E S

Copyright © 2000 by CCM Books, a division of CCM Communications

Published by Harvest House Publishers, Eugene, Oregon 97402

ISBN 0-7369-0444-1

Printed in the United States of America.

00 01 02 03 04 \IP/ 10 9 8 7 6 5 4 3 2 1

Jaci Velasquez is managed by Mike Atkins Management, Nashville, Tennessee

A publication of CCM Creative Ventures • Writer: Lindy Warren • **Art Direction & Design:** Susan Browne; Susan Browne Design • **Photography:** © Tony Baker Photography/MergeLeft

JACI VELASQUEZ

There are a lot better singers out there than me. I was in the right place in the right time that was God-ordained. I was willing and accepted God's plan. When you realize what God has for you, and accept that, you come into your own. And at that point, you become good at what you do.

Jaci Velasquez

WHEN trying to give some insight

into who Jaci Velasquez is, you could enlist numerous terms. She has been

called a child prodigy, teen phenom, role model for youth, Latin music's good

girl, and even a spunky salsera. You could go further by citing exact titles that

have characterized her at one time or another: Little Miss Texas, the Gospel

Music Association's New Artist of the Year (1997) and Female Vocalist of the

Year twice (1999 & 2000), and the only contemporary Christian artist ever nominated for a Grammy for Best Latin Pop Performance (January 2000). You might even consider her popularity among fans and the world at large: guest appearances on shows like the 2000 "Grammy Awards," "Donny & Marie," "The Today Show," the "1999 Latin Heritage Awards," and the "2000 ALMA Awards," as well as nine consecutive number one radio hits, two gold albums, and thousands of concert dates in the States and abroad.

But to really grasp who this 20-year-old Texas native is, you would need to plow through the terms and titles and the exhaustive list of accolades to her heart—for it is there where Jaci Velasquez lives. The small woman with the great big voice has mastered the delicate art of growing up while still clinging to the loves of her life: God, family (including Maltese puppy Dallas), music, people, her Spanish heritage, laughter, romance. Clearly, this fun-loving, passionate woman has caught a glimpse of the bigger story for her life—and it is that which defines Jaci Velasquez.

something different

F O R Jacqueline Davette Velasquez, attention has never been a rarity. From the day she was born, Oct. 15, 1979, in Houston, Texas, the freckled beauty with the waist-length chestnut hair has been at the center of the action. Jaci, the youngest of four, spent her childhood being doted on by her older siblings Mario, Julian and Dion.

Little Jacqueline Davette Velasquez begins
her journey on the road to success.

FROM THE VERY BEGINNING, SHE DIDN'T FIT INTO THE NORMAL MODE OF SCHOOL. SHE WAS ALWAYS MUCH MORE INTERESTED IN MUSIC. WHEN SHE WAS LITTLE, SHE WOULD LOOK OUT THE WINDOW AND WRITE A SONG. IT WAS JUST SOMETHING INBRED IN HER THAT SHE WAS GOING TO DO SOMETHING DIFFERENT.

DION LOPEZ, brother to jaci

WE'VE ALWAYS BEEN A REALLY CLOSE FAMILY, AND JACI WAS ONE OF THE BIGGEST JOYS IN OUR LIVES. MY BIG BROTHER, JULIAN, AND I WERE BESIDE OURSELVES WHEN WE FOUND OUT MY MOM WAS PREGNANT. I DIDN'T LET JACI OUT OF MY SIGHT. I WAS ALWAYS HOLDING HER, ALWAYS TAKING CARE OF HER, TELLING HER HOW PRETTY SHE WAS. FROM THE VERY BEGINNING, WE KNEW SHE HAD SOMETHING SPECIAL. —DION

The confidence of her big brothers plus the natural beauty of her mother, Diana (a former model), and the vocal strains of her father, David (formerly with gospel group The Galileans), led the child prodigy down the career path before she was old enough to talk.

SHE WAS IN HER CRIB, SNAPPING HER FINGERS, ON BOTH HANDS, IN TIME TO THE MUSIC. SHE COULDN'T DO IT VERY FAST, SO SHE WAS SNAPPING ON THE DOWNBEAT, EVERY FOUR COUNTS. I CALLED MY MOM AND TOLD HER TO COME LOOK AT THIS, AND WE COULDN'T BELIEVE IT. —JULIAN, BROTHER TO JACI

(LOS ANGELES TIMES)

CUTE AS A BUTTON

Jaci Velasquez, the early years

Always singing during the talent portion, Jaci won multiple beauty pageants, including Little Miss Texas. But the real showstopper came early on in a venue that through the years would become very familiar to the artist.

....

WHEN JACI WAS NOT EVEN 2, WE WERE AT CHURCH SINGING "OUR GOD REIGNS." SUDDENLY, THE PASTOR MOTIONED FOR US TO BE QUIET AND WE HEARD THIS LITTLE VOICE COMING FROM THE NURSERY. IT WAS JACI AND SHE WAS SINGING THE CHORUS. SO SINCE SHE WAS A BABY, I'VE KNOWN SHE WAS BEING CALLED TO DO SOMETHING BIG. —DIANA

....

That "something big" would mean many life changes for the Velasquezes in a few years. When Jaci was 10, David, a pastor at the time, announced his desire to go on the road as a traveling evangelist and musician—with his family in tow. But the idea seemed unrealistic. The family's bills were piling up and Diana, involved with the garment industry, had a high-paying job offer.

I JUST PRAYED AND FELT A PEACE ABOUT GOING ON THE ROAD. IT WAS A HARD DECISION BECAUSE WE KNEW IT WOULD MEAN TAKING JACI OUT OF SCHOOL, BUT SHE ADAPTED TO THE TRAVELING THING AMAZINGLY WELL. IT WAS LIKE SECOND NATURE. AT FIRST, WE WERE THERE JUST TO BE WITH DAVID, BUT SOON WE WERE DOING BACK-UP VOCALS FOR HIM. SO AS WE DROVE, HE'D TEACH US OUR PARTS. —DIANA

Songs weren't the only things learned in the backseat of the blue, four-door Honda Accord. Jaci was homeschooled via a VCR plugged into the car cigarette lighter. From fourth grade on, she learned English, math, science, and history through certified teachers on video. The set-up, while too atypical for some students, played out well with Jaci who, having practiced math and spelling with her older brothers, was always bored in the classroom.

WHEN SHE WAS IN THE FOURTH GRADE, I WALKED INTO HER ROOM AND SAW Xs THROUGH A CALENDAR HANGING ON HER WALL. SHE TOLD ME THAT THE Xs STOOD FOR THE DAYS SHE WAS GOING TO BE SICK—LITERALLY HALF THE YEAR. —DIANA

SHE WAS ALWAYS MUCH MORE INTERESTED IN MUSIC THAN SCHOOL. WHEN

SHE WAS LITTLE, SHE WOULD SING AND MAKE UP WORDS. WE HAVE A TAPE

OF HER SINGING, "EL SHADDAI, EL SHADDAI, ALL MY FRIENDS ARE MAD AT

ME." SHE WOULD LOOK OUT THE WINDOW AND WRITE A SONG. I THINK IT WAS

JUST SOMETHING INBRED IN HER THAT SHE WAS GOING TO DO SOMETHING

DIFFERENT. —DION

As the Velasquezes traveled from town to town, concert to concert, people began asking to hear more of their daughter. By age 12, David and Diana knew it was time to prepare her for solo flights.

....

WE JUST KEPT SEEING THE RESPONSE OF THE PEOPLE TOWARD HER, AND WE KNEW. IT GOT TO THE POINT WHERE PEOPLE WERE CALLING US BECAUSE THEY WANTED HER. —DIANA

....

While it might seem unlikely, the small woman with the big voice had no formal vocal training. When she was 5, she started piano lessons, but it would soon be apparent that Jaci's place would not be at a keyboard.

IT WAS SO FUNNY. THE TEACHER TOLD US, "IT'S BETTER IF SHE SINGS BECAUSE SHE TRIES TO SING EVERY NOTE, AND SHE'S MORE INTERESTED IN SINGING IT THAN PLAYING IT." SO WE GOT HER A VOCAL COACH, BUT SHE DIDN'T LIKE IT. AFTER THE FIRST TIME, SHE HID IN HER ROOM. SO WE JUST DECIDED THAT WASN'T GOING TO WORK EITHER. HER VOICE IS AN ACTUAL GOD-GIVEN TALENT. —DIANA

IF YOU COULD
SKYDIVE WITH
ANYONE? MY BIG
BROTHER JULIAN,
'CAUSE HE'S SO COOL.

FAVORITE PERSON
TO LAUGH WITH:
MY BROTHER DION, 'CAUSE
I LOVE IT WHEN I CAN GET
A LAUGH OUT OF HIM.

Taci Snapshots

THE family continued the hectic schedule of traveling and performing, with each date instilling more on-stage confidence in Jaci. For most Christian music vocalists, the next natural step would be a trip to Nashville to shop a record deal. But the Velasquezes never sought out a label.

I KNEW AFTER A COUPLE OF MINUTES THAT SHE
WAS THE ONE I WANTED TO SIGN. SHE WAS SO
AMAZING. SHE COMMANDED THE AUDIENCE AND HAD
THIS AMAZING POWER VOICE. I JUST SAW SOME-
THING I WAS VERY ATTRACTED TO.

JUDITH VOLZ, a&r director for word records

NOBODY WAS TRYING TO GET A RECORD DEAL. MY PARENTS WEREN'T EVEN TRYING. I KNEW CHRISTIAN MUSIC WAS ALWAYS SOMETHING I WANTED TO DO BECAUSE MUSIC HAS BEEN IN MY FAMILY FOREVER, BUT I NEVER THOUGHT I WOULD ACTUALLY BE DOING THIS. —JACI

The road to Nashville began unwinding with one song and one man's willingness to take a chance on an unknown. On a balmy afternoon in Houston, just as he was wrapping up a long day, Steve Seelig, on staff at First Baptist Church of Houston at the time, took a last-minute phone call from a woman gushing about the vocal prowess of a little Hispanic girl.

SHE SAID THIS GIRL SHOULD SING AT OUR CHURCH, AND SHE WAS VERY PERSISTENT. SO I LET HER COME AND DO ONE SONG ("NO ONE WILL EVER" FROM

RIBBONS AND BOWS

Pretty as a picture, young Jaci already has her dreams all wrapped up...

**ONE OF JACI'S CUSTOM RECORDS). I WAS BLOWN AWAY, AND I ASKED HER TO
COME BACK THE NEXT WEEK AND DO TWO SONGS. JACI WAS VERY CONFIDENT,
AND I COULD TELL SHE UNDERSTOOD MINISTRY. I SENSED SOMETHING VERY
SPECIAL ABOUT HER. SHE HAD DRIVEN IN WITH HER MOM AND DAD, AND THEY
WERE BARELY EKING OUT A LIVING. SHE WAS GOING FROM PLACE TO PLACE
FOR $50 A NIGHT. —STEVE SEELIG, FORMER BOOKING AGENT FOR JACI**

Impressed with her talent and authenticity, Seelig, then the booking agent
and manager for Point of Grace, helped the Velasquezes pull together a concert schedule for Jaci. Building on that, Seelig called well-known Nashville
manager Mike Atkins.

Jaci's debut album,
Heavenly Place, 1996

MIKE HADN'T EVEN HEARD HER, BUT HE SAID, "IF
YOU BELIEVE IN HER AND YOU'LL BOOK HER, I'LL
MANAGE HER." AFTER HE HEARD A TAPE AND MET
HER FAMILY, HE BEGAN SHOPPING A RECORD DEAL
FOR JACI. —STEVE SEELIG

Through Atkins, Judith Volz, then A&R director
for Myrrh Records, heard a tape of Jaci at age 12.

IT WAS PRETTY RAW, BUT I THOUGHT IF SHE SANG LIKE THAT AT 12 AND NOW

SHE WAS 14, THERE MIGHT BE SOMETHING HERE. AT THAT TIME, THERE WAS

A BIG HOLE IN THE MARKET FOR A YOUNG FEMALE. SO I WENT TO SEE HER AT

THIS LITTLE CHURCH IN HOUSTON. SHE CAME ON AND LOOKED REALLY CUTE

AND EXTREMELY NERVOUS. SHE OPENED WITH A SONG SHE SANG A CAPPELLA

IN SPANISH, AND I KNEW AFTER A COUPLE OF MINUTES SHE WAS THE ONE I

WANTED TO SIGN. SHE WAS SO AMAZING. SHE COMMANDED THE AUDIENCE

AND HAD THIS AMAZING POWER VOICE. TALKING WITH HER AND HER FAMILY

AFTER THE SHOW, I REALIZED THEY HAD A COMMITMENT TO EVANGELIZING. AT THAT TIME, I DON'T THINK SHE HAD A LOT TO SAY. HER DAD WAS DOING ALL THE TALKING, BUT SHE HAD BEEN WELL EDUCATED. I JUST SAW SOME-THING I WAS VERY ATTRACTED TO. I KNEW SHE HAD A GIFT. —JUDITH VOLZ

In the next four months, Jaci signed to Myrrh Records (label home to Amy Grant, Anointed, Fernando Ortega, Greg Long) at age 14 and released her label debut, *Heavenly Place,* two years later in 1996. In March 2000, Jaci switched record labels to Word Records when Volz, her first and only A&R director, moved from Myrrh to Word.

IN THE past four years, from age 16

to 20, Jaci has recorded four solo projects and is a regular on multi-artist

collections like *WoW 2000* and *Streams* (Word Records). In a sense, she's lived

the last four years of her life in record phases—from her Myrrh Records debut,

Heavenly Place (1996), and second project, simply titled *Jaci Velasquez* (1998),

to her ground-breaking Latin album, *Llegar A Ti* (1999), and *Crystal Clear*

(2000). With each work, she has come into a better understanding of

EVERY RECORD WITH HER HAS BEEN
FUN. EVERY RECORD IS AN EXPERIENCE.
YOU GO THROUGH A WHOLE LIFE
CYCLE IN ONE RECORD.

DION

Shining like the lights in L. A., Jaci's star gleamed brightly with five number one singles by the age of 18.

who she is as an artist and what she wants to communicate to her audience. Along the road, she has met multiple career-shaping influences, such as prolific producer Mark Heimermann (dcTalk, Amy Grant, Michael W. Smith). *Heavenly Place* started the symbiotic relationship between the two, and they have worked together ever since.

....

MARK TOOK HER UNDER HIS WING ON THE FIRST RECORD AND REALLY HELPED WITH FINDING THE SONGS AND DEVELOPING HER SOUND. SHE HAD BEEN INFLUENCED BY EVERYTHING FROM CINDY MORGAN TO WHITNEY HOUSTON, SO SHE HAD ALL KINDS OF INFLUENCES AND NO REAL SENSE OF HER OWN SOUND AND STYLE. THAT WAS A CHALLENGE AT 14 YEARS OLD. SHE WORKED SO WELL WITH HIM. SHE REALLY KIND OF CAME ALIVE IN THE STUDIO. —JUDITH VOLZ

....

SHE LOOKED LIKE A LITTLE GIRL BUT SOUNDED LIKE A WORLDLY, 30-YEAR-OLD WOMAN. WE HAD TO WORK ON THAT. —MARK HEIMERMANN, PRODUCER (LOS ANGELES TIMES)

Jaci resting comfortably... for the moment. Then it was back on the road for the busy teenager.

Heavenly Place (certified gold in 1998) produced five number one singles, including the first one, "If This World (the Na Na song)," "On My Knees," "Un Lugar Celestial," "We Can Make a Difference," and "Flower in the Rain." A year after the album released in '96, she won the Dove Award for New Artist of the Year. The second album, *Jaci Velasquez* (1998), brought its own set of challenges as Jaci, Heimermann, and Volz were faced with following up a hit debut. The team nailed it—from the premiere of the album's first single, "God So Loved," on "The 29th Annual Dove Awards" to the project's number one debut on Billboard sales charts. The album yielded four number one's and garnered her a Dove Award for Female Vocalist of the Year in '99. Pamela Muse, who has worked with Jaci throughout her career, remembers the road to the top:

....

WHEN I FIRST STARTED WORKING WITH JACI, SHE WASN'T ON TOUR WITH ANYONE. WE KIND OF ROLLED UP OUR SLEEVES AND SAID, "OKAY, WE NEED TO GO TO OKLAHOMA CITY BECAUSE THERE'S A GOOD BOOKSTORE THERE." SHE HAD THIS NEW SINGLE ("IF THIS WORLD"), AND IT WAS REALLY HOT. SO WE BEGAN DOING PROMOTIONAL THINGS LIKE CONTESTS AROUND THE SONG. WE PROBABLY WERE IN 15 CITIES THROUGH THE SUMMER. THEN SHE STARTED GETTING SOME CONCERT DATES AND BEFORE YOU KNEW IT, SHE ALREADY HAD HER SECOND SINGLE OUT. THEN BY THE TIME "ON MY KNEES" CAME OUT, IT WAS THERE. TWO YEARS LATER WHEN WE RETURNED WITH THE NEW ALBUM *(JACI VELASQUEZ)*, SHE WAS IN 33 CITIES IN TWO WEEKS.

—PAMELA MUSE, PUBLICIST FOR JACI

But the first two albums were shallow waters compared to the deep ocean she dove into on her third solo project, *Llegar A Ti*—the album she recorded to take to her culture. In '98, Jaci signed with Sony Discos—one of the world's leading Latin labels and home to pop icons like Jennifer Lopez and Ricky Martin—bringing life to a dream that surfaced long before Latin music exploded onto the U.S. pop scene in 1999 when Ricky Martin wowed an unsuspecting audience and world at the 1999 Grammys.

I've wanted to do a Latin record since I was a little girl. It was so important for everything to be authentic. I didn't want to just put out the same records translated into Spanish. I wanted authentic songs, producers, musicians, and I wanted the record to be authentically marketed to the Latin people. I've been singing in Spanish all my life. I did this album for my grandparents.

Jaci

The dream came to fruition. On the recommendation of Sony Discos President Oscar Llord, Jaci and Volz met with renowned Latin producer Rudy Perez, whose family had already told him about Jaci's Christian music work. Perez penned the first two singles from *Llegar A Ti* and adapted five songs from *Heavenly Place* to Spanish. Over the course of 14 months, Jaci and Volz worked on the project with Perez in Miami, trying out salsa rhythms and getting back to her Latin roots. Jaci, who doesn't speak Spanish fluently, had to learn the lyrics phonetically and be tutored in order to record the authentic album that doesn't have a lick of English on it.

....

WE HAD A WONDERFUL TIME WORKING ON THIS RECORD. RUDY WAS IN LOVE

WITH JACI'S VOICE, AND WE LOVED WORKING WITH OSCAR LLORD, WHO WAS

VERY HANDS-ON. HE CAME TO THE STUDIO ALMOST EVERY DAY TO LISTEN TO THE TRACKS. HE WAS EXTREMELY EXCITED ABOUT JACI AND BRINGING THIS KIND OF GIRL TALENT TO THE LATIN MARKETPLACE. —JUDITH VOLZ

....

The girl with the pretty smile and knock-you-over charisma attracted Llord's attention in 1997 during a Dove Awards performance.

....

WE'VE HAD A LOT OF FEMALE ARTISTS IN THE LATIN MARKET WHO ARE EXTREMELY EFFECTIVE IN DELIVERING RHYTHMIC SONGS. BUT I THINK THE CELINE DION OR WHITNEY HOUSTON TYPE OF VOICE IN THE LATIN MUSIC MARKET HAS NOT BEEN THERE LATELY. BUT JACI, WHO HAS ALREADY BEEN

Llegar A Ti

LARAS SPORTS AWARDS
(JACI MET ACTOR DYLAN MCDERMOTT (ABC-TV SHOW "THE PRACTICE"), WHO HAS SOMEWHAT REPLACED ANTONIO BANDERAS AS HER MOVIE HEARTTHROB).

"DONNY & MARIE"
SHOW PERFORMANCE

THE 2000 GRAMMYS
(I MET SHERYL CROW, AND I PRESENTED AN AWARD TO SANTANA.)

GRAMMY NOMINATION
FOR "BEST LATIN POP PERFORMANCE."

OPENING ACT FOR
BOTH RICKY MARTIN AND MARC ANTHONY.

DELIVERING PERFORMANCES IN THE FASHION SHE DOES, HAS A TREMENDOUS POTENTIAL TO GROW AND BECOME THAT SORT OF ARTIST IN OUR BUSINESS. —OSCAR LLORD, SONY DISCOS PRESIDENT (BILLBOARD)

Llegar A Ti, a watershed release in both the contemporary Christian music arena and the Latin world, yielded a number one song, the title track, on *Billboard*'s "Hot Latin Tracks" chart in '99, making her the only new artist to ever hit the chart's summit with a debut single. The album's second single, "Solu Tu," broke into the chart's top 10. During 1999, Jaci's face graced the covers of numerous magazines as she talked openly about her music and her faith.

I really believe the Latin market is my ministry because I'm reaching people who have no idea who Jesus Christ is. They think Christianity is a TV station. No, it's about a relationship with God. — Jaci

A little over a year after she released *Llegar A Ti*, Jaci came back with her third straight-ahead Christian record. For Jaci, *Crystal Clear* is a strong statement of faith.

jaci velasquez

JACI'S SELF-TITLED SECOND ALBUM, 1998

After coming off the Latin record, the one thing I really wanted to do with this new record was to make an album that would leave no doubt where I stood as a believer. —Jaci

....

WE PROBABLY LISTENED TO A COUPLE HUNDRED SONGS AT LEAST. JACI AND I HAVE ALWAYS BEEN GIRLS IN THE SENSE THAT WE LOVE SONGS THAT MOVE YOU TO EMOTION. I THINK THAT'S HOW OUR EXPERIENCE IN THE LATIN CULTURE INFLUENCED THIS RECORD. JACI IS AN AMAZING BALLAD SINGER, SO WE KNEW WE WANTED TO HAVE A GROUP OF TENDER, PASSIONATE BALLADS THAT MADE A STRONG STATEMENT. WE ALSO WANTED "UP" SONGS THAT WERE FUN AND DANCEABLE, BUT WITH MEATY LYRICS. THIS RECORD HAS BOTH TYPES, AND THERE'S NOT A LOT IN BETWEEN. —JUDITH VOLZ

Crystal Clear also represents a Jaci who has grown up and matured artistically. For the first time, she took a proactive approach to her record, partnering with Volz on the selection of songs and producers, and even producing her own vocals.

Crystal Clear is something I'm very proud of, and I think it's better than any record I've done. On Heavenly Place, *I was a 16-year-old doing a record. On* Crystal Clear, *I actually got to have a lot of input.* —Jaci

Jaci, who heretofore has interpreted other writers' songs, took a giant step forward on the new album, earning songwriting credits.

....

SHE'S MORE OF A WRITER THAN SHE THINKS SHE IS, BUT THIS IS THE FIRST TIME I ENCOURAGED HER TO WRITE. BEFORE, SHE ALWAYS TOOK A BACKSEAT. THIS TIME, WE DECIDED SHE HAD TO BE MY PARTNER ON THIS RECORD. I

DIDN'T WANT TO HAND HER SONGS ANYMORE. SHE'S GROWN UP. SHE DOES HAVE A SENSE OF WHAT SHE LIKES AND WHAT SHE WANTS TO SAY. WE HAND-PICKED THESE SONGS, AND I PULLED HER OFF THE ROAD TO GIVE HER TIME TO WRITE. AND WHAT SHE WROTE IS AMAZING. —JUDITH VOLZ

The album's first cut, "Escúche Me" ("Listen to Me"), is a collaboration between Jaci and Heimermann and an acknowledgement to her mom that the wise maternal counsel she received through the years has not returned void.

I wrote "Escúche Me" to pass on my Mom's advice to young girls, especially those who want to follow in my musical footsteps. I wish that before I got into this, people would have talked to me about things like saying something stupid in interviews. Instead, I had to learn the hard way and just figure it out myself. —Jaci

Rudy Perez, who worked with Jaci on *Llegar A Ti*, returned to produce and write songs for *Crystal Clear*. The man who has been integral in the music and the careers of Latin trailblazers like Jose Feliciano and Julio Iglesias, makes his English album songwriting debut with the cuts "Come as You Are," "Imagine Me Without You," and "Just a Prayer Away."

JACI'S SPANISH OFFERING, *Llegar A Ti*, 1998

JACI V

From bobby-soxer
to two-time Dove
Award winner for
Female Vocalist of
the Year.

SONG YOU WISH YOU'D WRITTEN:

BONNIE RAITT'S "I CAN'T MAKE YOU LOVE ME." IT'S REAL LIFE, YOU KNOW.

IF YOU COULD PERFORM WITH ANYONE: BONNIE RAITT. I RESPECT HER IN SO MANY WAYS. TALK ABOUT AN ARTIST WHO JUST STAYS TRUE TO HER ART.

Jaci Snapshots

no bustiers here

IN THE Latin world, she's been called "the young virgin with the angelic voice." And while Jaci is quick to laugh at the moniker, she is also proud of it. The description fits in well with her convictions and previous work with national youth organization True Love Waits, which promotes abstinence. In the past year, while promoting *Llegar A Ti*, her no-compromise attitude toward premarital sex and sensual clothing has become, in her words, her "ministry tool."

I want to communicate to little girls who are watching and trying to be like the girls they see on TV and in magazines that you don't have to wear bustiers or tight clothing. You don't have to show your belly button to be considered beautiful.

Jaci

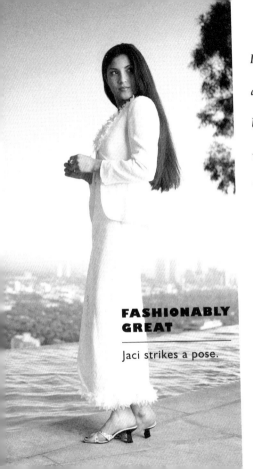

FASHIONABLY GREAT

Jaci strikes a pose.

In the Latin market, my stand for abstinence has probably been my biggest ministry tool. I've done interviews based solely on that subject. They know I'm a Christian. I don't slam it in their face, but it's very obvious. There, I think I'm perceived as the good girl, the angelic-type persona. If they really knew me, they'd know I'm not perfect at all. But that's the perception they have, which I'm very proud of. I like that I'm a good *girl. I keep my clothes on, but I'm still 20 years old. I love clothes, and I respect style. I want to communicate to little girls who are watching and trying to be like the girls they see on TV and in magazines that you don't have to wear bustiers or tight clothing. You don't have to show your belly button to be considered beautiful. —Jaci*

....

I WAS IN THE SONY DISCOS OFFICES A NUMBER OF TIMES WHEN SOMEONE WOULD BRING JACI CLOTHES OPTIONS THAT WERE OUTSIDE THE BOUNDARIES SHE THOUGHT WERE ACCEPTABLE. I SAT BACK IN THOSE MEETINGS AND WATCHED HER HOLD HER GROUND AND SAY TO SOME OF THE COMPANY PRESIDENTS, "I CAN'T CROSS THAT LINE BECAUSE MY AUDIENCE WOULDN'T UNDERSTAND THAT." I NEVER SAW ONE COMPROMISE. —JUDITH VOLZ

I'M REALLY PROUD OF HER THAT SHE'S WILLING TO STAND UP FOR WHAT SHE BELIEVES. THE EXAMPLE SHE PUTS FORTH IS REALLY NEEDED AMONG YOUTH. THEY'RE NOT GOING TO LISTEN TO AN ADULT, BUT THEY'LL LISTEN TO ANOTHER YOUNG PERSON. —DIANA

....

THE SPANISH RECORD HAS DEFINITELY BEEN HER BIGGEST CHALLENGE TO DATE BECAUSE THE PROMOTION OF IT WAS SO DIFFERENT THAN WHAT SHE WAS USED TO. THE PEOPLE EXPECT SOMETHING DIFFERENT, AND THEY DON'T KNOW EXACTLY WHAT SHE'S ABOUT. IT'S BEEN SO INTERESTING TO WATCH. SHE IS THE FIRST CONTEMPORARY CHRISTIAN ARTIST TO BREAK ON RADIO, TO HAVE A RECORD IN THE STORES, AND SHE'S CLOTHED. —DION

Still, the artist who is working hard to take Christ into unforged territory has faced criticism for her entrance into the Latin pop market, ironically by Christians in the culture.

JACI'S NEWEST,
Crystal Clear, 2000

It's the Christian Latin people who say, "You did a show with Chayanne, and he was in that movie with Vanessa Williams. Are you not a Christian anymore?" It's so bad because I believe I'm doing what the Bible says we're supposed to do. So if they want to criticize and question me, I just say, "So be it." I have to please God. This is what God's put in me, and if this is what His mission is for me, it's more important to please Him than to please man. That's a strong statement, but it's very true. —Jaci

I'M VERY PROUD BECAUSE I SEE SPIRITUAL GROWTH IN MY DAUGHTER. THE SKEPTICISM SHE'S ENDURED FROM CHRISTIANS IN THE LATIN WORLD HAS MADE HER STRONG IN HER STAND FOR KNOWING WHO SHE IS. I SEE THAT IN HER AND I'M AMAZED, AND YET I'M NOT. —DIANA

Llegar A Ti has already afforded her unprecedented opportunities to tell people about her faith both internally at Sony Discos and externally to the world at large.

I've actually witnessed to people in the company and my producer. I'm not telling people, "You have to believe this or you're going to hell." I pray that my life is a testimony, but that I'm also able to tell them a little about the Gospel without shoving it down their throats. —Jaci

FAVORITE BOOK:

LIFE ON THE EDGE
(FOCUS ON THE FAMILY)
BY DR. JAMES DOBSON
I LOVE THAT BOOK.

**FAVORITE WEB
SITE TO SURF:**

SUPERESTRA.COM (97.3 OUT
OF LOS ANGELES). IT'S A
GREAT HISPANIC RADIO
STATION SO I GO TO THE
SITE TO LISTEN TO IT.

Jaci Snapshots

the cost

WHILE it's true that the life of a musician or celebrity does embody a certain glamour and glitz, any artist is quick to say that the 15 minutes of fame do not match the amount of work involved in climbing to the top of the hill and staying there. So is the case with Ms. Velasquez, who runs on Power Bars and giant lattes 24/7. She is the consummate hardworking artist, and she has the frequent flyer miles (200,000 in '99), bus trips, and hotel reservations to prove it.

If life could have gone exactly the way I wanted it to, I would have started this the day I finished high school and be exactly where I am today. But it didn't happen that way, and that's okay because it's just how God planned it, and I'm cool with that.

Jaci

OUR FAMILY HAS SEEN SOME REALLY GOOD TIMES AND SOME REALLY HARD TIMES. AT TIMES, THERE WAS LITTLE OR NO MONEY COMING IN AND IT WAS EVEN UNCERTAIN IF THERE WOULD BE ANY GIFTS UNDER THE TREE. JACI WAS SHIELDED FROM THAT AS MUCH AS POSSIBLE, BUT SHE RECOGNIZED THE HARDSHIP. THAT'S WHERE SHE LEARNED TO LIVE LIFE ON THE EDGE, WORK HARD AND HAVE FUN. —DION

....

I HAVE A GREAT RESPECT FOR JACI'S UNBELIEVABLE WORK ETHIC. I DON'T KNOW OF AN ARTIST I'VE WORKED WITH NOR HEARD ABOUT WHO WORKS AS HARD AS SHE DOES. THAT REQUIRES A SENSE OF RESPONSIBILITY AND COMMITMENT TO WHAT YOU'RE DOING AND TO THE PEOPLE YOU'RE DOING IT FOR. —JUDITH VOLZ

YOU NEVER HEAR HER COMPLAIN ABOUT BEING ON THE ROAD TOO LONG OR IN A HOTEL SHE DOESN'T LIKE. THIS IS HER LIFE. THIS IS WHAT SHE DOES. I'LL WAKE HER UP AT 3 A.M., AND SHE GETS RIGHT UP AND GETS GOING. —DIANA

....

I TELL JACI ALL THE TIME: "BABY, THERE ARE TWO KINDS OF ARTISTS—THE ONES WHO CAN'T GET A GIG TO SAVE THEIR LIFE AND THEY'RE FIGHTING TO STAY ALIVE AND THE ONES WHO ARE SO SUCCESSFUL THAT AT TIMES, IT DOESN'T SEEM LIKE THEY HAVE A LIFE. EITHER WAY, IT'S THE SAME SITUA-TION. YOU'RE EITHER WORKING HARD TO GET SOMETHING YOU DON'T HAVE OR YOU'RE FIGHTING HARD TO DO EVERYTHING PEOPLE WANT YOU OR NEED YOU TO DO. YOU HAVE TO DECIDE WHAT KIND OF ARTIST YOU ARE." JACI HAS CHOSEN TO WORK VERY, VERY HARD. —DION

61

But for the girl who grew up working, the airplanes, buses, performances, interviews, photo shoots, and meetings are all just a part of life.

I guess because I grew up into it, then it's weird for me to stay home. That's just real life. You hop on a bus, you hop on a plane, and you go. You live out of a suitcase. What's the big deal? It's normal. I love people so I don't mind it, but I could live without a few things like hotels. I get real tired of hotels. —Jaci

Still, Jaci and everyone around her know that many sacrifices have been made for the life and career she has today. While the work and its results are rewarding, the cost has been high. Her graduation day was a privately held ceremony and her high school prom was as a date at someone else's milestone event.

....

HAS SHE MISSED A LOT OF HER LIFE? TONS OF HER LIFE. AND THAT'S WHAT

PEOPLE OUT THERE HAVE A HARD TIME REALIZING—JUST EXACTLY HOW MUCH

OF YOUR LIFE YOU GIVE UP. HER GETTING A PICTURE OF HERSELF IN HER CAP

AND GOWN MEANT MORE THAN ANY RECORD COVER OR PHOTO IN A MAGAZINE.

SHE WAS SO PROUD OF THAT. SHE SENT IT OUT TO EVERYONE SHE KNEW. —DION

....

Obviously I'm aware of the fact that I did miss a normal childhood. If life could have gone exactly the way I wanted it to, I would have started this the day I finished high school and be exactly where I am today. But it didn't happen that way, and that's okay because it's just how God planned it, and I'm cool with that. —Jaci

Unfortunately, with the hard work and career comes scrutiny and backbiting.

After the first record hit, people were out to find something. I've learned that just as soon as people love to see you succeed, they love to see you fail. They wait for it. A year ago, I was having lunch with my brother and one of his friends. A lady from a record label saw me and called my management, accusing me of drinking. My brother's friend had a drink, and it appeared that I was drinking. Those kind of things upset me so badly. They cut deep. —Jaci

IN *living* COLOR

LITTLE PRINCESS

Jaci started winning hearts and stealing
the show from the very beginning...

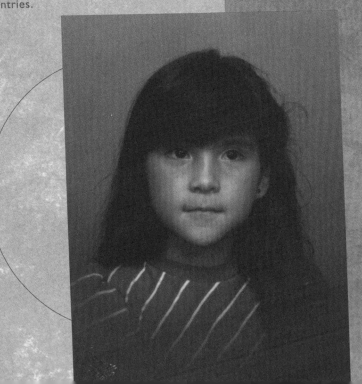

SCHOOL DAZE

Jaci poses for the obligatory yearbook entries.

FAMILY REUNION

Jaci with David and Diana Velasquez,
the guiding influences in her life.

Celebrating 12 years of hard work, Jaci trades in the stage and microphone for a cap and gown.

The whole family comes out to celebrate Jaci's success.

The Velasquezes
enjoy a winter
wonderland.

It's crystal clear that
the camera loves Jaci.

Mrs. V. and her little angel.

IN *living* COLOR ←——————————————————————→

FAVORITE COFFEE:

SPECIAL COFFEE DRINKS:
WHITE CHOCOLATE MOCHA;
DAY-TO-DAY AT MY HOUSE:
STARBUCKS WITH VANILLA
CREAM. (I MAKE GREAT
COFFEE.)

FAVORITE VACATION:

BARCELONA, SPAIN WITH
MOM, DAD, DION, AND ME.
I LOVED EVERY MINUTE OF
IT. MY FAVORITE PART WAS
THE FOOD. THE CITY WAS
BREATHTAKING.

Jaci Snapshots

beyond a shadow of a doubt

IT'S CLEAR to anyone who

spends more than five minutes with Jaci and her mother, Diana, that this

familial relationship has created a certain bond. Diana—whose dark,

laughing eyes and sweet nature are no doubt the source for Jaci's striking

looks and passion for life—has nurtured her daughter from day one and con-

tinues, in her own words, to "love on" her daughter.

SHE KNOWS I'M THERE AND THAT I LOVE HER NO MATTER WHAT. IF SHE MESSES UP, I STILL LOVE HER. IF SHE FEELS SICK AND CAN'T SING, I STILL LOVE HER. SHE KNOWS I LOVE HER BEYOND A SHADOW OF A DOUBT.

DIANA

SHE KNOWS I'M THERE AND THAT I LOVE HER NO MATTER WHAT. IF SHE MESSES UP, I STILL LOVE HER. IF SHE FEELS SICK AND CAN'T SING, I STILL LOVE HER. SHE KNOWS I LOVE HER BEYOND A SHADOW OF A DOUBT. —DIANA

....

And that love translates into tangible acts as mother's intuition kicks in and antennae go up.

....

I PRAY FOR HER ALL THE TIME. WHEN SHE'S ON STAGE, I'M BACK THERE PRAYING FOR HER. I CAN READ HER LIKE NO ONE ELSE CAN. IF A SITUATION COMES UP WHERE SHE SEEMS UNCOMFORTABLE, SHE CAN GIVE ME A LOOK AND I KNOW EXACTLY WHAT SHE'S FEELING. ONLY A MOTHER CAN DO THAT. —DIANA

....

Like mother,
like daughter

My mom's my best friend. She's about the only person who really knows every-thing about me. When I got my first kiss, I told her about it. —Jaci

Those around Jaci credit much of her career success and her commitment to hard work to her parents.

....

I THINK A LOT OF JACI'S WORK ETHIC CAN BE ATTRIBUTED TO HER PARENTS.

HER MOTHER'S BEEN OUT ON THE ROAD WITH HER NONSTOP SINCE JACI WAS

14. WHEN SHE DID SIGN WITH US AND COMMIT TO A CAREER OF THIS KIND,

SHE HAD PARENTS THERE WHO HELD HER UP AND CONTINUED TO TEACH HER.

—JUDITH VOLZ

....

The bond continues to strengthen, even when life changes. In May 2000, the 20-year-old songstress moved out of her parents' Nashville home and into her own two-story, four-bedroom house. The mother/daughter tie, however, grows tighter in new ways.

NOW THAT SHE'S GETTING OLDER, I'M FINDING WE'RE GETTING EVEN CLOSER. I DIDN'T THINK THAT WAS POSSIBLE. SHE'S BECOMING A WOMAN AND I CAN RELATE TO HER THAT WAY. WHEN WE WENT TO HAWAII, I THOUGHT, "I'M GOING TO GIVE HER A LITTLE SPACE AND LET HER HANG OUT WITH THE GUYS IN THE BAND." SO I WOULD GET UP EARLY AND GO INTO THE OTHER PART OF THE SUITE. PRETTY SOON, SHE WAS CALLING OUT, "MOM, WHERE ARE YOU?" WE HUNG AROUND TOGETHER AND GOT EVEN CLOSER ON THAT TRIP. —DIANA

HERO:

MY MOM

**FAVORITE THING
TO DO WITH MOM:**

SHOP, DRINK COFFEE,
AND READ BOOKS.

**FAVORITE MOTHER'S
DAY MEMORY:** WHEN I WAS 12,
MY MOM'S FAVORITE THING FOR ME TO
WEAR WAS THIS RED DRESS. SO I SAVED
MY MONEY, WORE THAT DRESS, AND
HAD A PROFESSIONAL PHOTOGRAPH
MADE THAT I GAVE TO HER ON
MOTHER'S DAY. SHE LOVED IT!

Jaci Snapshots

livin' la vida normal

FOR JACI Velasquez, the majority

of life is not the typical life of a 20-year-old. But through the years, and

especially lately since purchasing her own two-story home in May 2000,

the girl who has lived in the spotlight has found a way to enjoy the simple

pleasures in life.

It's a good thing when you have people in your life who understand you and like you for who you are. In the past year, whenever I got into a bad mood and was the diva for 10 minutes, my band could see past me and tell me, "Stop."

Jaci

Having been homeschooled, Jaci missed her own prom. But two years ago, she flew to Houston to be a friend's prom date. It must have been important. She turned down the opportunity to perform at a Billy Graham crusade to wear a corsage and dance the night away. She has since sung at several crusades, including San Antonio's Alamo Dome, in front of 60,000 people.

I'm a real person. I just never get to do anything real. The prom was really cool.

I danced the whole night and had a great time. —Jaci

In Nashville she attends Belmont Church and when she's not on the road or the stage, you'll find her shopping (her favorite pastime), taking pictures (another hobby), watering the multiple beds of flowers in her spacious back-yard garden, sitting in her Old World-style living room complete with hard-wood floors and antique candelabra, or playing with Dallas, her Maltese named after a kitten her brother had while attending Southern Methodist University in Dallas.

"Since I bought my house, I'm doing things I never thought I would do in life. I love the garden so I spend time pulling weeds. I'm doing the normal things like washing dishes except they're my dishes now, and doing laundry."

The new role of homeowner, she says, is a sign that Jaci Velasquez is growing up. "I wanted to buy my own house because it was time for me to grow up, to just say, 'I have to be a big girl now.'"

....

SHE'S GROWN UP REALLY WELL. I THINK 18 WAS PROBABLY THE HARDEST

YEAR FOR HER. SHE WAS CAUGHT IN THE FACT THAT ONCE SHE TURNED 18,

PEOPLE THOUGHT, "WELL, YOU'RE MATURE. YOU CAN'T MAKE MISTAKES." I

THINK THAT IN THE LAST COUPLE OF YEARS SHE HAS BEEN ABLE TO SEE A

LOT. —JUDITH VOLZ

....

Jaci candidly admits that growing up wasn't something she welcomed and embraced. "Who wants to leave the life you've been born into?" she says. "I feel like I've been a 13-year-old for the past five years and in the last six months, I've had to suddenly grow up."

But age does have its perks, especially in the area of building relationships. This incredibly poised, strikingly beautiful young woman admits that the subject of male companionship is one of her favorite topics.

When do I not like to talk about dating? Yes, it's true. I like boys probably more than I should. I didn't start dating until I was 17. I've had like two, three boyfriends in my life. My first was at 17 and the second was at 19, and both were long relationships. I've managed to stay good friends with all the guys I've dated, and that's really important. When solid friendship isn't part of the relationship, dating tends to just be about kissing. —Jaci

For her, the lack of social interaction on the road has been hard on developing relationships and friendships.

I didn't have a normal childhood so I never built relationships. I'm very immature when it comes to relationships and how people perceive me. It's really cool to have those best friends in life. It's hard sometimes for me to have girl best friends. I grew up with my brothers, so I'm used to having guys around. But I'm not one of those girls who needs guys' attention to be happy. —Jaci

Dove Awards Honor Rich Mullins • A Delirious Invasion • Fred Hammond's Double Play

CONTEMPORARY CHRISTIAN MUSIC

ccm

MAGAZINE

The wonder years of

Jaci Velasquez

A personal glimpse behind the eyes of Christian music's teen phenom.

June 1998

Jaci first graced the cover of
CCM MAGAZINE in June 1998.

Her friends and the people who surround her keep her grounded, she says. "It's a good thing when you have people in your life who understand you and like you for who you are. In the past year, whenever I got into a bad mood and was the diva for 10 minutes, my band could see past me and tell me, 'Stop.'"

FAVORITE FOOD: BESIDES MY MOM'S COOKING, SUSHI.

FAVORITE FLOWER: STARGAZER LILIES

FAVORITE TIME OF DAY: DUSK

FAVORITE PLACE IN THE WORLD: MY LIVING ROOM BECAUSE IT'S MINE. EVERYTHING THAT'S IN HERE IS BECAUSE I CHOSE FOR IT TO BE HERE. I CAN GET AWAY FROM THE WORLD IN THIS ROOM.

Taci Snapshots

WHILE the work ethic and musical career are ever-present in the life of Jaci Velasquez, standing at the forefront is the reason behind the vocational efforts. The girl who at age 5 walked to the front of the crowd at an area camp crusade to accept Christ as her Savior feels she has been called to stand onstage and tell others about Christ. But, she says, it's only been in the past two years that her relationship with her Creator has become hers.

"In the last couple of years I've come into my own relationship with God," she says. "I read the Bible because I want to know, not because my parents are watching to keep me accountable. I keep myself accountable." With that new outlook, her relationship with Christ has evolved and changed.

I've come to a place where I talk to God because I feel like He's the one person in the world who really understands. He has become my best friend. It's so easy to say that. I know. I've said that before. But now I can truly say, "He's my best friend, and I want to learn from Him." —Jaci

Clearly, the past two years of this 20-year-old's life exemplify how maturity breeds depth and wisdom.

I like to think of myself as trying to be as close as I can to who David was. He messed up so many times, but he was a man after God's own heart. And that's what I want to be. I don't want to ask for God's forgiveness to keep me from going to hell if I were to die in the next 10 minutes. I don't want my relationship with Him to be born out of self-satisfaction. I want to know that God has forgiven me for what I've done wrong. That's what I'm striving for right now in my walk with Him. —Jaci

FAVORITE SCRIPTURE:

ROMANS 1:16,17

FAVORITE BOOK OF THE BIBLE:

ESTHER

Jaci Snapshots

future roads

LOOKING ahead, the future seems

bright for Jaci Velasquez. In fall 2000, she's on a 60-city tour with Plus One

(*Crystal Clear* tour), the first tour to feature her as the headlining artist.

This tour is really exciting for me because it's mine, and I've gotten to really make decisions. They bring staging ideas to me. Plus One is doing a lot of great things. I'm really proud of them because they're making waves. —Jaci

....

SHE LOOKS AT THIS NEW TOUR AS A NEW CHAPTER IN HER LIFE. SHE'S BEEN THROUGH X AMOUNT OF THINGS WITH THE LATIN RECORD, AND SHE'S LOOKING SO FORWARD TO GETTING ON A BUS AND DOING WHAT SHE DOES. —DIANA

No doubt, the artists and crew of the *Crystal Clear* tour will be in for a wallop of a good time with Miss V making the decisions. "It's going to be fun," she laughs. "You've got a 20-year-old coming up with where we're going to eat, what we'll do after the show."

After the tour, Jaci has plans to begin work on a Spanish spiritual album for Sony Discos. And, she says, one day she hopes to act. That could be a reality since scripts come pouring in with acting offers. However, the right one has yet to come her way.

....

SO FAR, WE HAVEN'T FOUND THE RIGHT ROLE. THEY ALWAYS HAVE A LOVE SCENE IN THEM, AND THAT'S NOT SOMETHING JACI WANTS TO DO. —MIKE ATKINS, JACI'S MANAGER

She plans to attend college one day, though her current schedule won't allow it, and in the long-term, after about 10 years, she says, Jaci has aspirations beyond solo artistry.

....

One day, I want to produce records for other people. I want to get out of the artist thing at some point, and I want to get into producing other young female artists. I have a heart for them. —Jaci

Steven Curtis Chapman

VeggieTales

Russ Taff

Out of Eden

MUSIC, FAITH & CULTURE

CCM

SUMMER MUSIC PREVIEW

Hope Floats
Inside *Streams*, summer's
biggest project

$3.00 USA $4.95 CAN

www.ccmagazine.com

Jaci again makes the cover of CCM MAGAZINE as one of the artists on the popular *Streams* project. (June 1999)

IF I WEREN'T A SINGER, I'D BE:

A MAKEUP ARTIST/
STYLIST

**FAVORITE
MOVIE:**

THE CROW

**FAVORITE PLACE
TO SHOP:**

NEIMAN MARCUS
IN DALLAS

Jaci Snapshots

decorations

IN HER short career, Jaci Velasquez

has racked up numerous awards, accolades and career achievements that have

allowed her to communicate the message of the gospel in churches, arenas,

and TV studios as well as on the airwaves. She is quickly becoming one of

Christian music's most decorated female artists.

DISCOGRAPHY

2000   **CRYSTAL CLEAR**

1999   **LLEGAR A TI**

1999   **CLIPS AND CONVERSATIONS**
(video)

1998   **JACI VELASQUEZ**

1996   **HEAVENLY PLACE**

VIDEO HISTORY

NINE CONSECUTIVE NUMBER ONE CHRISTIAN RADIO SONGS

"If This World" (*Heavenly Place*)

"On My Knees" (*Heavenly Place*)

"Glory" (*Jaci Velasquez*)

"Un Lugar Celestial" (*Heavenly Place*)

"We Can Make a Difference" (*Heavenly Place*)

"Speak for Me" (*Jaci Velasquez*)

"Flower in the Rain" (*Heavenly Place*)

"God So Loved" (*Jaci Velasquez*)

"Show You Love" (*Jaci Velasquez*)

CHART HISTORY

BILLBOARD MAGAZINE NUMBER ONE "HOT LATIN TRACKS" AND "LATIN POP" CHARTS:

"Llegar A Ti" (*Llegar A Ti*)

"Llegar A Ti" was the only debut single from any new artist to hit the number one spot on *Billboard's* "Hot Latin Tracks" chart in 1999, and made Jaci the first contemporary Christian music artist to ever hold the chart's top position.

ACHIEVEMENTS

RIAA CERTIFIED GOLD (500,000 IN SALES) RECORDS: HEAVENLY PLACE, JACI VELASQUEZ

JACI VELASQUEZ DEBUTED AT NUMBER ONE ON BILLBOARD'S "CONTEMPORARY CHRISTIAN" SALES CHART, SPENDING SIX WEEKS AT NUMBER ONE. THE ALBUM CHARTED AT NUMBER 54 ON THE "BILLBOARD 200" SALES CHART.

HEAVENLY PLACE SPENT **83 WEEKS ON BILLBOARD'S "HEATSEEKERS" CHART.**

HER FIRST TWO ALBUMS, HEAVENLY PLACE AND JACI VELASQUEZ, HAVE **SOLD MORE THAN 1.6 MILLION COPIES COMBINED.**

JACI WAS THE **FOURTH TOP-SELLING TEENAGE FEMALE ARTIST** IN THE UNITED STATES IN SEPTEMBER '98.

JACI WAS THE FIRST ARTIST TO REPRESENT THE NASHVILLE COMMUNITY AND THE CHRISTIAN MUSIC INDUSTRY WITH A NOMINATION IN THE **"BEST LATIN POP PERFORMANCE" CATEGORY OF THE GRAMMY AWARDS 2000.**

JACI HAS BEEN A **GUEST COLUMNIST** FOR CAMPUS LIFE MAGAZINE.

JACI **CO-HOSTED THE 2000 TEJANO MUSIC AWARDS** ON UNIVISION TV.

JACI HAS **AUTHORED** A HEAVENLY PLACE (SIMON & SCHUSTER).

SPOKESPERSON FOR THE NATIONAL CHRISTIAN COLLEGE ASSOCIATION AND PARABLE CHRISTIAN STORES.

JACI HAS BEEN THE SUBJECT OF ARTICLES IN NUMEROUS MAGAZINES AND NEWSPAPERS, SUCH AS LATIN MUSIC MAGAZINE (COVER), TEEN PEOPLE, TEEN BEAT, CCM MAGAZINE (COVER), LATIN GIRL (COVER), CAMPUS LIFE (COVER), TODAY'S CHRISTIAN WOMAN, GUIDEPOSTS FOR TEENS, BRIO, (COVER), THE TENNESSEAN, WASHINGTON POST, NEW YORK DAILY NEWS, DALLAS MORNING NEWS, MINNEAPOLIS STAR TRIBUNE, HOUSTON CHRONICLE, ATLANTA JOURNAL CONSTITUTION AND SEATTLE TIMES, AMONG OTHERS.

MEDIA APPEARANCES

SHE HAS ALSO MADE A MULTITUDE OF TV APPEARANCES, INCLUDING THE 2000 GRAMMY AWARDS PRETELECAST ON VH1, "ALMA AWARDS," "TEJANO MUSIC AWARDS," "LATIN HERITAGE AWARDS," "BILLBOARD LATIN MUSIC AWARDS," "CBS THIS MORNING," "THE TODAY SHOW," "THE 700 CLUB," "GOOD MORNING TEXAS," DOVE AWARDS ('97-'99), TARGET COMMERCIAL.

AWARDS/HONORS

DOVE
2000 FEMALE VOCALIST OF THE YEAR

DOVE
2000 SPANISH LANGUAGE ALBUM OF THE YEAR

DOVE
2000 SPECIAL EVENT ALBUM OF THE YEAR
(STREAMS)

DOVE
1999 FEMALE VOCALIST OF THE YEAR

DOVE
1998 "SONG OF THE YEAR"
("ON MY KNEES")

DOVE 1997
NEW ARTIST OF THE YEAR

CCM MAGAZINE'S READER'S POLL
1997 BEST NEW ARTIST

NOMINATIONS

<u>GRAMMY</u> **2000 "BEST LATIN POP PERFORMANCE"**

BILLBOARD MUSIC VIDEO AWARD:
1998 ("GOD SO LOVED")

BILLBOARD MUSIC VIDEO AWARD:
1997 ("UN LUGAR CELESTIAL")

<u>DOVE</u> **2000 SPECIAL EVENT ALBUM OF THE YEAR**
(BRIDGES: SONGS OF UNITY AND PURPOSE)

<u>DOVE</u> **1999 ARTIST OF THE YEAR**

<u>DOVE</u> **1999 SONG OF THE YEAR**
("GOD SO LOVED")

<u>DOVE:</u> **1999 SPECIAL EVENT ALBUM OF THE YEAR**
(TOUCHED BY AN ANGEL: THE ALBUM)

<u>DOVE</u> **1999 POP/CONTEMPORARY RECORDED SONG OF THE YEAR**
<u>("GOD SO LOVED")</u>

<u>DOVE</u> **1998 FEMALE VOCALIST OF THE YEAR**

<u>DOVE</u> **1997 FEMALE VOCALIST OF THE YEAR**

<u>DOVE</u> **1997 INSPIRATIONAL SONG OF THE YEAR**
<u>("ON MY KNEES")</u>

<u>DOVE</u> **1997 POP/CONTEMPORARY ALBUM OF THE YEAR**
<u>(HEAVENLY PLACE)</u>

YOU CAN VISIT JACI AT
www.planetjaci.com

WRITE TO JACI AT
P.O. Box 3568
Brentwood, TN 37204